Money Moves: Navigating the Urban Economic Landscape

Lara Andrew

Copyright © [2023]

Title: Money Moves: Navigating the Urban Economic Landscape
Author's: Lara Andrew

All rights reserved. No part of this publication may be reproduced, stored in a retrieval system, or transmitted in any form or by any means, electronic, mechanical, photocopying, recording, or otherwise, without the prior written permission of the publisher or author, except in the case of brief quotations embodied in critical reviews and certain other non-commercial uses permitted by copyright law.

This book was printed and published by [Publisher's: **Lara Andrew**] in [2023]

ISBN:

TABLE OF CONTENT

Chapter 1: Understanding the Urban Economic Landscape   07

Introduction to Urban Economics

The Impact of Urbanization on the Economy

Key Players in the Urban Economic Environment

Chapter 2: Economic Challenges in Urban Areas   13

Income Inequality and Poverty

Unemployment and Job Opportunities

Housing Affordability and the Cost of Living

Chapter 3: Urban Economic Development   19

Urban Planning and Economic Growth

Attracting and Retaining Businesses in Urban Areas

Revitalizing Declining Urban Neighborhoods

Chapter 4: The Role of Government in Urban Economics 26

Government Policies and Urban Economies

Taxation and Economic Development

Public Infrastructure and Urban Economic Growth

Chapter 5: Urbanization and Sustainable Development 33

Balancing Economic Growth and Environmental Sustainability

Urban Agriculture and Food Security

Sustainable Transportation and Infrastructure

Chapter 6: Entrepreneurship and Innovation in Urban Economies 40

The Role of Startups in Urban Economic Development

Technology and Innovation Hubs in Urban Areas

Supporting Small Businesses in Urban Environments

Chapter 7: Urban Economic Opportunities for All 46

Inclusive Economic Development Strategies

Enhancing Financial Literacy in Urban Communities

Creating Economic Opportunities for Marginalized Groups

Chapter 8: Navigating the Urban Job Market 52

Job Search Strategies in Urban Areas

Skills and Education for Urban Employment

Thriving in the Gig Economy: Urban Freelancing

Chapter 9: Investing in the Urban Economy 58

Real Estate Investment in Urban Areas

Stock Market and Urban Economic Trends

Impact Investing and Socially Responsible Urban Development

Chapter 10: Financial Planning for Urban Living 64

Budgeting and Managing Urban Living Expenses

Saving and Investing in an Urban Environment

Retirement Planning in the Urban Setting

Chapter 11: Overcoming Financial Challenges in the Urban Landscape 70

Dealing with Urban Debt and Financial Stress

Strategies for Overcoming Urban Financial Barriers

Building Resilience in the Face of Urban Economic Challenges

Chapter 12: The Future of Urban Economics 76

Emerging Trends and Technologies in Urban Economies

Forecasting the Future of Urban Development

Creating Sustainable and Equitable Urban Economies

Chapter 1: Understanding the Urban Economic Landscape

Introduction to Urban Economics

Welcome to the fascinating world of urban economics! In this subchapter, we will delve into the fundamental concepts and principles that underpin the economic environment of our cities. Whether you are a student, a professional, or simply curious about the dynamics of urban economies, this introduction will provide you with a solid foundation to navigate the urban economic landscape.

Urban economics is the study of how cities function and the economic forces that shape them. Every day, millions of people interact with the urban environment, whether through work, housing, transportation, or leisure activities. Understanding the economic factors that drive these interactions is crucial to comprehending the complexities and opportunities that cities offer.

One of the key aspects of urban economics is the concept of agglomeration. Cities are not just random clusters of people and buildings; they are centers of economic activity that attract individuals, firms, and industries. The agglomeration effect arises from the benefits that result from proximity and density, such as increased productivity, knowledge spillovers, and a wider range of goods and services. By understanding how agglomeration shapes urban economies, we can better grasp the dynamics of urban growth and development.

Moreover, urban economics explores the role of land and real estate in cities. Land is a finite resource, and its scarcity in urban areas gives rise to unique economic phenomena, such as skyrocketing property prices and the need for efficient land-use planning. The intricate relationship between land, housing markets, and the allocation of resources is a crucial aspect of urban economics, with significant implications for both individuals and policymakers.

Transportation is another vital component of urban economics. Efficient transportation systems are the lifeblood of cities, enabling the movement of goods, services, and people. The study of transportation economics provides insights into the challenges of urban mobility, congestion, and the design of sustainable transportation networks.

Lastly, urban economics also encompasses the examination of urban inequality and poverty. Cities are often characterized by stark disparities in income, education, and access to opportunities. Understanding the root causes of urban inequality and devising effective policies to address these challenges are essential for creating inclusive and vibrant cities.

In conclusion, this introduction to urban economics offers a glimpse into the fascinating field that explores the economic environment of cities. By studying the concepts and principles of urban economics, you will gain a deeper understanding of the forces that shape our urban spaces and the opportunities and challenges they present. Whether you are an economist, a urban planner, or simply an individual curious about the world around you, this subchapter will equip you with valuable knowledge to navigate the complex urban economic landscape.

The Impact of Urbanization on the Economy

Urbanization has become a defining characteristic of the modern world. As more and more people flock to cities in search of better opportunities, the impact of this phenomenon on the economy cannot be ignored. In this subchapter, we will explore the various ways in which urbanization influences the economic environment and affects the lives of individuals and communities.

One of the most significant impacts of urbanization on the economy is the creation of job opportunities. Cities act as magnets, attracting businesses and entrepreneurs who seek to tap into the vast market potential that urban areas offer. The concentration of industries and businesses in cities leads to increased employment opportunities for individuals, ultimately driving economic growth. Moreover, urban areas provide a fertile ground for innovation and creativity, which fuels the development of new industries and technologies, further boosting the economy.

However, the rapid pace of urbanization can also pose challenges to the economy. As cities become more crowded, competition for resources and infrastructure becomes more intense. Inefficient urban planning and inadequate investment in public services and utilities may result in congestion, pollution, and inadequate housing. These issues not only impact the quality of life of urban dwellers but also hinder economic productivity. Therefore, it is crucial for policymakers and urban planners to address these challenges and ensure sustainable and inclusive urban development.

Furthermore, urbanization also influences consumer behavior and spending patterns. The proximity of various goods and services in cities makes it easier for individuals to access a wide range of products. As a result, urban areas become hubs of consumption, driving economic activity. Additionally, the diversity and density of urban populations create opportunities for niche markets and specialized businesses to thrive, catering to the unique needs and preferences of urban dwellers.

In conclusion, urbanization has a profound impact on the economy, both positive and negative. While it creates job opportunities and fosters innovation, it also presents challenges related to infrastructure and resource management. As cities continue to grow, it is crucial to prioritize sustainable and inclusive urban development to ensure that the economic benefits of urbanization are shared by all. By understanding the impact of urbanization on the economy, individuals, policymakers, and businesses can navigate the urban economic landscape more effectively and contribute to the overall well-being of society.

Key Players in the Urban Economic Environment

In the rapidly evolving urban economic landscape, understanding the key players is crucial for anyone interested in navigating the complexities of the city's financial ecosystem. This subchapter will provide an overview of the key players in the urban economic environment and shed light on their roles, influence, and impact on the overall economic health of a city.

Government entities play a significant role in shaping the urban economic environment. They create policies, regulations, and incentives that guide economic activities and promote growth. Local government bodies, such as city councils and mayors' offices, are responsible for setting the vision and direction for economic development. They create strategic plans, attract businesses, and foster an environment conducive to entrepreneurship and innovation. State and federal governments also play a role through funding initiatives, tax incentives, and infrastructure development.

Businesses and corporations are crucial players in the urban economic environment as they drive job creation, investment, and economic growth. Large corporations often have a significant impact on the local economy, influencing market trends, and providing employment opportunities. Small and medium-sized enterprises (SMEs) are also vital contributors to the urban economic landscape. They bring diversity, innovation, and vitality to the city, creating a dynamic business environment.

Financial institutions are key players in the urban economic environment. Banks, credit unions, and other financial entities provide the necessary capital for businesses and individuals to invest, expand, and prosper. They offer loans, mortgages, and financial services that facilitate economic transactions and stimulate growth. Furthermore, financial institutions also support economic development initiatives, such as affordable housing programs or small business loans, which can have a transformative impact on urban communities.

Non-profit organizations and community-based initiatives are essential components of the urban economic environment, especially in underserved communities. These organizations focus on community development, job creation, and poverty alleviation. They provide crucial resources, support, and services to individuals, families, and businesses, fostering economic resilience and social stability.

Lastly, individuals themselves are key players in the urban economic environment. Their skills, creativity, and entrepreneurial spirit contribute to the vibrancy and dynamism of the city's economy. By participating in the labor market, spending, saving, and investing, individuals shape the economic landscape and influence market trends.

Understanding the roles and interactions of these key players is essential for anyone navigating the urban economic environment. By recognizing the contributions and objectives of each player, individuals, businesses, and policymakers can work together to create a thriving, inclusive, and sustainable urban economy for everyone.

Chapter 2: Economic Challenges in Urban Areas

Income Inequality and Poverty

In today's urban economic landscape, income inequality and poverty are two pressing issues that affect everyone. The economic environment we live in has a significant impact on our lives, influencing our opportunities, well-being, and future prospects. Understanding the causes and consequences of income inequality and poverty is essential for everyone, as it shapes the social fabric of our communities and the overall health of our economy.

Income inequality refers to the unequal distribution of income among individuals or households within a society. It is a complex issue influenced by various factors such as education, skills, discrimination, and social mobility. While some degree of income inequality is expected in any economy, extreme disparities can have detrimental effects on society. High levels of income inequality can lead to social unrest, increased crime rates, and reduced social mobility.

Poverty, on the other hand, is a state of deprivation in which individuals or households lack the basic necessities of life, such as food, shelter, and healthcare. Poverty can be both a cause and a consequence of income inequality. Those who are born into poverty often face limited opportunities for education and employment, perpetuating the cycle of poverty across generations.

The consequences of income inequality and poverty are far-reaching. They affect not only those directly impacted but also society as a whole. Research has shown that societies with higher levels of income inequality tend to have lower levels of social trust, lower life expectancy, and higher rates of mental health issues. Poverty limits individuals' ability to access quality education and healthcare, hindering their chances of upward social mobility and perpetuating societal divides.

To address income inequality and poverty effectively, it is crucial for everyone to be aware of these issues and actively engage in finding solutions. Governments, policymakers, and communities play a vital role in implementing policies that promote economic equality, such as progressive taxation, investment in education and skills training, and social safety nets. Additionally, individuals can contribute by supporting organizations that provide assistance to those in need, volunteering their time and skills, and advocating for policies that reduce income disparities.

In conclusion, income inequality and poverty are not isolated issues affecting only a specific group of individuals. They impact everyone in the economic environment we live in. Understanding the causes and consequences of income inequality and poverty is essential for creating a more equitable society and ensuring a prosperous future for all. By working together, we can navigate the urban economic landscape and make significant strides towards reducing income disparities and eradicating poverty.

Unemployment and Job Opportunities

In today's rapidly changing economic environment, understanding the dynamics of unemployment and job opportunities is crucial for everyone. The global economy has experienced significant shifts, leading to both positive and negative implications for individuals and communities. In this subchapter, we will explore the complexities of unemployment and the various job opportunities that exist in the urban economic landscape.

Unemployment is a persistent challenge faced by societies worldwide. It not only affects individuals but also has broader implications for the economic environment. High unemployment rates can contribute to social unrest, economic instability, and a decline in overall living standards. However, it is important to note that unemployment is not solely a result of individual shortcomings, but rather a reflection of larger systemic issues.

To navigate the urban economic landscape effectively, it is crucial to understand the factors that contribute to unemployment. Technological advancements, globalization, and economic recessions are some of the key drivers in job loss and unemployment. Automation and artificial intelligence have significantly impacted certain industries, leading to job displacement. Globalization has created new opportunities but has also resulted in the outsourcing of jobs, particularly in manufacturing sectors.

While unemployment can be daunting, it is essential to recognize that job opportunities continue to emerge within the urban economic landscape. As certain industries decline, new sectors and job roles evolve. The digital economy, for example, has created a demand for skills in data analysis, digital marketing, and software development. Additionally, the renewable energy sector offers job opportunities in fields such as solar installation, wind turbine maintenance, and energy efficiency consulting.

Adapting to the changing job market requires individuals to develop and enhance their skillsets continuously. Lifelong learning and upskilling are crucial in staying relevant and competitive. Governments, educational institutions, and private organizations play a vital role in providing training programs and resources to support individuals in acquiring new skills.

Furthermore, entrepreneurship and self-employment have become increasingly popular avenues for job creation. The rise of the gig economy and the ability to leverage technology to start one's own business present opportunities for individuals to take control of their financial futures.

In conclusion, understanding the complexities of unemployment and job opportunities is essential for navigating the urban economic landscape. By recognizing the underlying factors contributing to unemployment and embracing emerging job sectors, individuals can position themselves to thrive in a rapidly changing economy. Lifelong learning, upskilling, and entrepreneurial endeavors are crucial in adapting to the evolving job market. It is important for individuals, governments, and organizations to work collaboratively to ensure that everyone has access to job opportunities and the necessary resources to succeed in the economic environment.

Housing Affordability and the Cost of Living

In an era of growing urbanization, one of the most pressing issues faced by people from all walks of life is the ever-increasing cost of living, particularly in terms of housing affordability. As cities expand and populations rise, the economic environment is undergoing significant changes, leading to a surge in housing prices and a subsequent decline in affordability. This subchapter aims to shed light on the challenges faced by individuals and families in finding affordable housing and navigating the complex urban economic landscape.

The cost of housing has skyrocketed in recent years, outpacing wage growth and making it increasingly difficult for individuals and families to find affordable homes. This issue is not confined to any particular socio-economic group; it affects everyone, from low-income individuals struggling to make ends meet to middle-class families trying to secure a comfortable living space. As a result, the dream of homeownership has become an unattainable reality for many, with a significant portion of people resorting to renting, often at exorbitant prices.

Several factors contribute to the rising housing costs. Urbanization and population growth place a strain on available housing stock, driving up demand and prices. Additionally, limited land availability, zoning regulations, and the cost of construction materials further exacerbate the affordability crisis. As a consequence, individuals find themselves allocating a significant portion of their income towards housing, leaving little room for savings or other essential expenses.

To address this issue, it is crucial for policymakers, urban planners, and community leaders to prioritize affordable housing initiatives. This can include the development of affordable housing units, implementing rent control measures, and promoting mixed-income neighborhoods. Additionally, increased investment in public transportation and infrastructure can help alleviate the burden of high housing costs by allowing individuals to live farther away from city centers while still maintaining access to employment opportunities.

Furthermore, individuals must understand and explore alternative housing options, such as cooperative housing, shared living arrangements, and micro-housing solutions. These alternatives can provide affordable and sustainable living spaces, fostering a sense of community and reducing the strain on individual budgets.

In conclusion, the issue of housing affordability and the cost of living is an urgent concern within the economic environment of urban areas. The rising housing costs affect everyone, from low-income individuals to middle-class families. To tackle this challenge, a multifaceted approach involving policy changes, investment in infrastructure, and exploring alternative housing options is necessary. By addressing housing affordability, we can ensure that individuals and families have access to safe, affordable housing and can navigate the urban economic landscape more successfully.

Chapter 3: Urban Economic Development

Urban Planning and Economic Growth

In today's rapidly evolving economic environment, urban planning plays a crucial role in fostering economic growth and development. The decisions made in urban planning not only shape the physical landscape of cities but also pave the way for economic opportunities and prosperity for its residents. This subchapter explores the intricate relationship between urban planning and economic growth, highlighting the importance of thoughtful and strategic approaches to city development.

Cities are the engines of economic growth, attracting businesses, investments, and a skilled workforce. Effective urban planning ensures that cities are designed and organized in a manner that optimizes economic activities. By creating well-designed infrastructure, such as transportation networks, utility systems, and public spaces, urban planners can facilitate the efficient movement of goods, services, and people within cities. This, in turn, enhances productivity and enables businesses to thrive.

Moreover, urban planning can unlock the potential for economic growth by attracting private investments. When cities are planned with a clear vision and long-term goals, it instills confidence in investors, encouraging them to commit their resources to urban development projects. This influx of private capital stimulates economic growth, creates job opportunities, and improves the overall quality of life for residents.

Beyond attracting investments, urban planning also addresses social and environmental concerns, which are essential for sustainable economic growth. By incorporating mixed-use development, green spaces, and affordable housing, urban planners can create vibrant communities that promote social equity and inclusivity. These factors contribute to a higher quality of life for residents and attract a diverse and skilled workforce, further fueling economic growth.

However, urban planning is not without its challenges. Rapid urbanization, limited resources, and changing demographic trends require planners to adapt their strategies constantly. It is crucial for urban planners to engage with local communities, businesses, and policymakers to ensure that planning decisions align with the needs and aspirations of the people. Collaboration and stakeholder involvement are key to successfully navigating the complex urban economic landscape.

In conclusion, urban planning is an integral component of economic development. By creating well-designed cities that attract investments, promote social equity, and prioritize sustainability, urban planners can foster economic growth and improve the overall economic environment. As we navigate the dynamic economic landscape, it is imperative to understand the critical role that urban planning plays in shaping prosperous and resilient cities for everyone.

Attracting and Retaining Businesses in Urban Areas

In today's rapidly evolving economic landscape, urban areas have become the epicenter of business growth and innovation. With an ever-increasing demand for jobs and economic opportunities, cities must constantly strive to attract and retain businesses to ensure a thriving economic environment. This subchapter explores the key strategies and considerations for attracting and retaining businesses in urban areas.

One of the primary factors that businesses consider when deciding to establish or relocate their operations is the availability of a skilled workforce. Urban areas, with their diverse population and access to educational institutions, often have a competitive advantage in this regard. By investing in education and training programs, cities can enhance their talent pool and make themselves more attractive to businesses seeking skilled employees.

Infrastructure plays a crucial role in attracting businesses to urban areas. A reliable and efficient transportation system, including well-maintained roads, public transportation, and access to airports and ports, is essential for businesses to thrive. Additionally, cities must invest in modern and sustainable infrastructure, such as high-speed internet, to meet the needs of businesses in the digital age.

To create a business-friendly environment, cities should streamline regulations and reduce bureaucratic red tape. Simplifying the process of obtaining permits and licenses can greatly encourage businesses to set up shop in urban areas. Furthermore, offering incentives and tax breaks to businesses that invest in the local community can be a powerful tool for attracting and retaining businesses.

Collaboration between the public and private sectors is vital for fostering a favorable business environment. By engaging with local businesses and industry leaders, cities can gain insights into their needs and challenges. This collaboration can lead to the development of tailored programs and initiatives that attract businesses and support their growth and development.

Lastly, a vibrant and inclusive urban culture is crucial for attracting and retaining businesses. Cities that offer a high quality of life, with amenities such as parks, cultural institutions, and a diverse culinary scene, can be highly attractive to businesses and their employees. Additionally, promoting diversity and inclusion in the workforce can create an environment that fosters innovation and creativity.

In conclusion, attracting and retaining businesses in urban areas requires a multifaceted approach that addresses the needs of businesses, employees, and the community. By focusing on factors such as skilled workforce, infrastructure, business-friendly regulations, collaboration, and a vibrant urban culture, cities can create an economic environment that attracts and retains businesses, leading to sustained growth and prosperity for all.

Revitalizing Declining Urban Neighborhoods

In recent years, declining urban neighborhoods have become a significant concern in many cities. Economic downturns, population shifts, and neglect have led to the deterioration of once vibrant areas, resulting in a multitude of social and economic challenges. However, there is hope on the horizon as communities and policymakers recognize the importance of revitalizing these neighborhoods to create a thriving urban economic environment.

Revitalizing declining urban neighborhoods is crucial for several reasons. Firstly, these neighborhoods hold a rich cultural heritage and historic significance that should be preserved and celebrated. Neglecting these areas not only erases a part of a city's identity but also hampers its potential for growth and development. Secondly, revitalization efforts can create new economic opportunities, attract investment, and generate jobs, leading to a more prosperous city as a whole. Moreover, improving the quality of life in these neighborhoods can enhance social cohesion and reduce crime rates, fostering a sense of community and belonging.

To effectively revitalize declining urban neighborhoods, a multi-faceted approach is required. It begins with comprehensive urban planning that takes into account the unique characteristics and needs of each neighborhood. Engaging community members in the decision-making process ensures that their voices are heard, and their concerns are addressed. This participatory approach fosters a sense of ownership and empowers residents to actively contribute to the revitalization efforts.

Investment in infrastructure is another essential element of revitalization. Upgrading roads, sidewalks, parks, and public spaces not only improves the physical environment but also attracts businesses, residents, and visitors. Creating mixed-use developments that include affordable housing, commercial spaces, and community amenities can breathe new life into declining neighborhoods and provide opportunities for small businesses to thrive.

Furthermore, addressing education and healthcare disparities is crucial in revitalization efforts. Investing in schools, community centers, and healthcare facilities can improve access to quality education and healthcare services, which are essential for social mobility and well-being. Providing training programs and support for local entrepreneurs and businesses can also contribute to economic growth and job creation within the neighborhood.

Revitalizing declining urban neighborhoods is a complex and long-term process that requires collaboration between residents, policymakers, and various stakeholders. It demands patience, creativity, and sustained investment. However, the benefits of revitalization extend far beyond the borders of the neighborhood itself. A thriving urban economic environment can positively impact the entire city, attracting new residents, businesses, and opportunities.

In conclusion, revitalizing declining urban neighborhoods is essential for creating a prosperous urban economic environment. By preserving their cultural heritage, generating economic opportunities, and enhancing quality of life, cities can ensure a more inclusive and sustainable future for all. It is a collective responsibility to invest in the revitalization of these neighborhoods, as the success of our cities depends on the success of every neighborhood within them.

Chapter 4: The Role of Government in Urban Economics

Government Policies and Urban Economies

In today's rapidly changing economic environment, it is essential to understand the crucial role that government policies play in shaping urban economies. Government policies can have a profound impact on the growth, development, and sustainability of cities, directly influencing the economic opportunities available to individuals and businesses.

One of the primary objectives of government policies is to promote economic growth and create a conducive environment for businesses to thrive. Through various measures such as tax incentives, infrastructure development, and regulatory frameworks, governments can attract investments and foster entrepreneurship. By implementing policies that support innovation and provide a skilled workforce, urban economies can become hubs of technological advancements and attract high-paying jobs.

Moreover, government policies also aim to address socioeconomic inequalities and ensure inclusive growth. By implementing targeted programs and initiatives, governments can uplift marginalized communities and provide them with equal access to economic opportunities. This not only promotes social justice but also contributes to the overall economic vibrancy of a city. It is crucial for policymakers to design policies that address the specific needs of different communities within an urban setting to create a fair and inclusive economy.

Furthermore, government policies play a vital role in creating sustainable urban economies. With increasing concerns about climate change and resource depletion, it is imperative for governments to prioritize environmentally friendly policies. By investing in renewable energy, promoting green infrastructure, and implementing sustainable transportation systems, cities can transition towards a low-carbon economy. These policies not only reduce the impact on the environment but also create new green jobs and attract sustainable businesses.

However, it is important to note that government policies are not without challenges. Striking a balance between economic growth and environmental sustainability, addressing the needs of diverse communities, and ensuring effective implementation are just some of the hurdles faced by policymakers. It is crucial for governments to engage in extensive research, consult with experts, and actively involve stakeholders to develop comprehensive policies that benefit all segments of society.

In conclusion, government policies have a profound impact on urban economies. By implementing measures to promote economic growth, address socioeconomic inequalities, and create sustainable cities, governments can shape thriving and inclusive urban economic landscapes. It is essential for individuals, businesses, and policymakers to understand the interplay between government policies and urban economies to navigate the ever-changing economic environment successfully.

Taxation and Economic Development

Taxation plays a crucial role in shaping the economic environment of any nation. It is a powerful tool used by governments to generate revenue, redistribute wealth, and promote economic development. In this subchapter, we will explore the intricate relationship between taxation and economic development, shedding light on its impact on individuals, businesses, and the overall economic landscape.

At its core, taxation is a means of funding government expenditures. The revenue generated through taxes enables governments to provide essential public goods and services, such as infrastructure, education, healthcare, and social welfare programs. These investments are vital for fostering economic development and improving the quality of life for citizens.

Taxation also acts as a mechanism for redistributing wealth and reducing income inequality. Progressive tax systems, where individuals with higher incomes pay a higher tax rate, contribute to a more equitable distribution of wealth. By taxing the affluent more heavily, governments can provide support to the less privileged, thereby reducing poverty and promoting social cohesion.

Moreover, tax policies can be designed to incentivize specific economic activities and sectors. Lower tax rates or tax incentives can encourage businesses to invest, innovate, and expand their operations. For instance, offering tax breaks to companies engaging in research and development can spur technological advancements and drive economic growth.

However, it is essential to strike a balance when implementing tax policies. Excessive taxation can stifle economic development by burdening individuals and businesses, hindering investment, and dampening consumer spending. High tax rates can discourage entrepreneurs from starting new ventures and hinder job creation. Therefore, it is crucial for policymakers to carefully consider the potential impact of tax measures on economic growth and development.

Furthermore, the efficiency and fairness of tax systems play a critical role in economic development. Transparent and well-designed tax systems, with clear rules and minimal bureaucracy, promote business confidence and attract foreign investment. Simultaneously, ensuring that tax burdens are distributed fairly among different income groups fosters social stability and encourages economic participation.

In conclusion, taxation and economic development are intricately linked. Through taxation, governments can fund public services, reduce income inequality, and incentivize economic activities. However, the design and implementation of tax policies must be carefully considered to strike the right balance between generating revenue and promoting economic growth. By creating efficient and fair tax systems, governments can navigate the urban economic landscape, fostering sustainable development and improving the economic environment for everyone.

Public Infrastructure and Urban Economic Growth

In today's rapidly evolving economic environment, the role of public infrastructure in fostering urban economic growth cannot be overstated. Public infrastructure refers to the basic physical and organizational structures needed to support the functioning of a community, including transportation systems, utilities, public spaces, and social infrastructure. These amenities form the backbone of any thriving urban center, attracting businesses, residents, and tourists alike.

Investing in public infrastructure is crucial for creating a favorable economic environment. Well-designed transportation networks, such as roads, bridges, and public transit systems, facilitate the movement of goods, services, and people, reducing congestion and improving productivity. They enhance connectivity between neighborhoods, cities, and regions, making it easier for businesses to access markets, suppliers, and a diverse workforce. Similarly, reliable utilities, including water, electricity, and telecommunications, are essential for businesses to operate efficiently and for residents to enjoy a high quality of life.

Public spaces, such as parks, plazas, and recreational facilities, contribute to the social and cultural vibrancy of a city. They provide venues for community events, promote physical and mental well-being, and attract visitors. A well-maintained and accessible social infrastructure, such as schools, hospitals, and libraries, supports human capital development, ensuring a skilled workforce and a healthy population. These components collectively create an attractive environment that encourages businesses to invest, residents to stay, and tourists to explore.

Moreover, public infrastructure investment has a multiplier effect on the economy. Construction projects generate employment opportunities, creating jobs for both skilled and unskilled workers. The increased economic activity resulting from infrastructure development boosts local businesses, from suppliers of construction materials to retail and hospitality sectors. Additionally, improved infrastructure can raise property values, leading to increased tax revenues for governments to invest back into the community, further fueling economic growth.

However, it is not enough to focus solely on building new infrastructure. The maintenance and modernization of existing assets are equally important for sustained urban economic growth. Neglecting maintenance can lead to infrastructure deterioration, increasing costs in the long run and hindering economic activity. Rather than solely expanding infrastructure, policymakers must prioritize regular upkeep and technological advancements to ensure that existing assets remain efficient and relevant.

In conclusion, public infrastructure plays a pivotal role in shaping the economic environment of urban areas. By investing in transportation systems, utilities, public spaces, and social infrastructure, cities can attract businesses, residents, and tourists, creating a virtuous cycle of economic growth. Furthermore, infrastructure investment generates employment, stimulates local businesses, and increases tax revenues. However, it is essential to balance expansion with maintenance to ensure the long-term viability of these assets. Ultimately, a well-developed and maintained public infrastructure is the bedrock upon which thriving urban economies are built.

Chapter 5: Urbanization and Sustainable Development

Balancing Economic Growth and Environmental Sustainability

In today's rapidly industrializing world, the pursuit of economic growth often takes center stage, but at what cost? As we strive to propel our cities and nations forward, it's crucial to recognize the delicate balance between economic progress and environmental sustainability. This subchapter aims to shed light on this critical issue, exploring the ways in which we can navigate the urban economic landscape while preserving and nurturing our natural surroundings.

Economic growth is undeniably essential for the prosperity of any society. It creates jobs, boosts incomes, and improves living standards. However, this growth often comes at the expense of our environment. The extraction of natural resources, the emission of greenhouse gases, and the pollution of air, water, and soil are just a few of the consequences of unchecked economic expansion. These actions not only degrade our surroundings but also pose long-term risks to human health and well-being.

To strike a balance between economic growth and environmental sustainability, we must adopt a holistic and conscientious approach. Governments, businesses, and individuals all have a crucial role to play in this endeavor.

Government policies and regulations are instrumental in ensuring sustainable economic growth. By implementing stringent environmental standards, promoting renewable energy sources, and incentivizing eco-friendly practices, governments can steer economic activities towards a greener path. Moreover, fostering collaboration between public and private sectors can lead to innovative solutions that prioritize both economic advancement and environmental protection.

Businesses, too, must embrace corporate social responsibility by integrating sustainable practices into their operations. Adopting green technologies, reducing waste, and implementing environmentally friendly policies not only contribute to environmental preservation but also enhance a company's reputation and competitiveness. Embracing sustainability can lead to long-term profitability while mitigating environmental harm.

As individuals, we hold immense power to drive change. By making conscious choices in our daily lives, such as reducing energy consumption, embracing sustainable transportation options, and supporting environmentally conscious businesses, we can collectively create a significant impact. Additionally, engaging in community initiatives, advocating for stronger environmental regulations, and raising awareness among friends and family can help foster a culture of sustainability.

The pursuit of economic growth should not come at the expense of our planet's health. By striving for a harmonious balance between economic progress and environmental sustainability, we can create a future where economic growth supports, rather than undermines, the well-being of both people and the planet. It is through collective effort, collaboration, and conscious decision-making that we can navigate the urban economic landscape while safeguarding our economic environment for generations to come.

Urban Agriculture and Food Security

In recent years, the concept of urban agriculture has gained significant attention due to its potential to address food security concerns in urban areas. As the world becomes increasingly urbanized, it is crucial to explore innovative solutions to ensure access to nutritious and affordable food for everyone. This subchapter will delve into the topic of urban agriculture and its role in creating a sustainable and secure food system within the urban economic environment.

Urban agriculture refers to the practice of growing, processing, and distributing food within cities or urban areas. It encompasses a range of activities, including rooftop gardens, community gardens, vertical farming, and aquaponics. By utilizing underutilized spaces such as vacant lots, rooftops, and indoor environments, urban agriculture presents a unique opportunity to enhance food production and reduce the distance between food sources and consumers.

One of the primary benefits of urban agriculture is its contribution to food security. By cultivating food in close proximity to urban dwellers, it reduces the reliance on long supply chains and decreases the vulnerability to disruptions in the global food system. Additionally, urban agriculture can increase the availability of fresh produce, particularly in food deserts where access to nutritious food is limited. This not only improves the physical health of individuals but also has positive implications for the overall economic well-being of the community.

Moreover, urban agriculture can generate economic opportunities within the urban environment. By creating local jobs in farming, processing, and distribution, it contributes to the growth of a diversified urban economy. Furthermore, urban agriculture can foster entrepreneurship and innovation, particularly in areas such as vertical farming and aquaponics. These emerging technologies not only increase food production but also provide opportunities for urban farmers to generate income while addressing environmental sustainability.

However, the implementation of urban agriculture faces several challenges. Limited access to land, lack of infrastructure, and regulatory barriers pose significant hurdles for individuals and communities interested in engaging in urban farming. Therefore, it is essential for policymakers and urban planners to facilitate the development of supportive policies and provide necessary resources to promote the growth of urban agriculture.

In conclusion, urban agriculture holds immense potential to enhance food security and create a sustainable and secure food system within the urban economic environment. By utilizing innovative farming practices and utilizing underutilized spaces, urban agriculture can address the challenges of food access and contribute to the economic growth of urban areas. However, it requires collaborative efforts from policymakers, urban planners, and individuals to overcome the barriers and harness the benefits of urban agriculture for the economic well-being of everyone.

Sustainable Transportation and Infrastructure

In today's rapidly urbanizing world, the need for sustainable transportation and infrastructure has become increasingly important. As cities continue to grow and expand, there is a pressing need to create efficient and environmentally-friendly systems that can accommodate the needs of a growing population while minimizing the negative impact on the economic environment.

Transportation is a crucial aspect of any urban environment, as it connects people, goods, and services. However, traditional modes of transportation, such as private cars, are not sustainable in the long run. They contribute to traffic congestion, air pollution, and carbon emissions, which harm both the environment and the economy. To address these challenges, cities around the world are adopting sustainable transportation solutions.

One of the most effective ways to promote sustainable transportation is by investing in public transportation systems. Efficient and reliable public transit networks, including buses, trams, and trains, can significantly reduce the number of private vehicles on the road. This not only reduces traffic congestion but also decreases greenhouse gas emissions and improves air quality. Additionally, public transportation provides affordable mobility options for all residents, regardless of their income level, contributing to a more equitable urban environment.

Another important aspect of sustainable transportation is the promotion of non-motorized modes of transport, such as walking and cycling. Investing in pedestrian-friendly infrastructure, such as sidewalks and bike lanes, encourages people to choose these sustainable modes of transportation for short trips. Not only does this reduce the reliance on cars, but it also promotes a healthier lifestyle and fosters a sense of community within neighborhoods.

In addition to sustainable transportation, it is crucial to invest in sustainable infrastructure. This includes the development of green buildings, renewable energy systems, and efficient waste management systems. Green buildings, for example, are designed to reduce energy consumption and minimize environmental impact, leading to cost savings for both residents and businesses. Renewable energy systems, such as solar and wind power, can provide clean and sustainable sources of energy, reducing dependence on fossil fuels.

Furthermore, efficient waste management systems, including recycling and composting programs, can help reduce landfill waste and promote a circular economy. These initiatives create new jobs, reduce pollution, and conserve resources, contributing to a healthier and more sustainable economic environment.

In conclusion, sustainable transportation and infrastructure are crucial components of a thriving urban environment. By investing in public transportation, promoting non-motorized modes of transport, and developing sustainable infrastructure, cities can create more efficient, equitable, and environmentally-friendly systems. These initiatives not only benefit the environment but also contribute to a healthier and more prosperous economic environment for everyone. It is essential for individuals, businesses, and governments to collaborate and prioritize sustainability to ensure a sustainable and resilient future.

Chapter 6: Entrepreneurship and Innovation in Urban Economies

The Role of Startups in Urban Economic Development

In recent years, startups have emerged as a driving force behind urban economic development. These innovative ventures, often led by young entrepreneurs, have the potential to transform the economic landscape of cities and create a thriving business environment. This subchapter will explore the crucial role that startups play in urban economic development and highlight the positive impact they have on the economic environment.

Startups are known for their ability to disrupt traditional industries and introduce new products, services, and business models. They are highly adaptable and quick to respond to changing market demands, which makes them ideal drivers of economic growth in urban areas. As these startups grow, they create jobs, attract investment, and contribute to the overall economic prosperity of the city.

One of the key ways startups contribute to urban economic development is through job creation. Unlike established corporations, startups often hire young and talented individuals who bring fresh perspectives and new ideas to the workforce. By providing employment opportunities, startups help reduce unemployment rates, increase income levels, and improve the overall quality of life in the city.

Furthermore, startups attract investment from venture capitalists, angel investors, and government funding agencies. This influx of capital stimulates economic activity, as it allows startups to expand their operations, invest in research and development, and scale their businesses. The increased investment not only benefits the startups themselves but also creates a ripple effect in the local economy, leading to the growth of supporting industries and the creation of even more jobs.

Startups also foster a culture of innovation and entrepreneurship, which has a profound impact on the economic environment of a city. They encourage collaboration, knowledge sharing, and networking among entrepreneurs, leading to the formation of startup ecosystems and innovation hubs. These ecosystems bring together startups, investors, mentors, and support organizations, creating a vibrant ecosystem that nurtures entrepreneurship and fosters economic growth.

In conclusion, startups play a vital role in urban economic development. Through their ability to disrupt industries, create jobs, attract investment, and foster innovation, startups contribute to the economic wellbeing of cities. It is essential for policymakers, investors, and the community at large to recognize and support the growth of startups, as they hold the potential to transform urban economies and create sustainable prosperity for all.

Technology and Innovation Hubs in Urban Areas

In recent years, urban areas have witnessed a rapid rise in the development of technology and innovation hubs. These hubs have become the epicenter of economic growth, transforming the urban landscape and attracting a diverse range of businesses and individuals. This subchapter explores the significance of technology and innovation hubs in urban areas and their impact on the economic environment.

Technology and innovation hubs are vibrant ecosystems that foster the growth of startups, entrepreneurs, and established companies. They provide a conducive environment for collaboration, knowledge sharing, and networking among like-minded individuals. These hubs are typically located in urban areas as they offer access to a large pool of talent, infrastructure, and resources.

One of the primary benefits of these hubs is the creation of jobs and economic opportunities. They attract high-skilled professionals and entrepreneurs who contribute to the local economy through job creation and innovation. The presence of technology and innovation hubs often leads to the establishment of ancillary businesses such as cafes, restaurants, and service providers, further boosting the economic environment.

Moreover, these hubs act as catalysts for urban revitalization. They breathe new life into underutilized spaces, transforming them into vibrant communities. By attracting a diverse range of individuals, technology and innovation hubs contribute to the social and cultural fabric of urban areas.

Furthermore, these hubs play a crucial role in fostering collaboration between academia, industry, and government. Universities and research institutions often collaborate with technology hubs to commercialize their research and ideas, leading to the development of groundbreaking innovations. This collaboration not only benefits the individual entities involved but also strengthens the overall economic ecosystem.

Additionally, technology and innovation hubs drive innovation and competitiveness on a global scale. They attract international talent, investment, and partnerships, enhancing the reputation of the city and positioning it as a global leader in technology and innovation. This global recognition further attracts businesses and individuals, creating a positive feedback loop of economic growth.

In conclusion, technology and innovation hubs in urban areas have revolutionized the economic environment. They create jobs, foster collaboration, drive innovation, and contribute to the overall revitalization of urban areas. By understanding the significance of these hubs, policymakers, businesses, and individuals can harness their potential to navigate the urban economic landscape successfully. Whether you're an entrepreneur looking to start a business or an individual seeking economic opportunities, technology and innovation hubs are the places to be.

Supporting Small Businesses in Urban Environments

In today's rapidly evolving economic landscape, small businesses play a critical role in shaping urban environments. They contribute to the local economy, create job opportunities, and add vibrancy to the fabric of our cities. However, these businesses often face unique challenges in urban settings, making it essential for us to come together and support their growth and sustainability.

Urban environments offer a plethora of opportunities for small businesses. The diverse customer base, high foot traffic, and access to resources can be advantageous, but they can also be overwhelming. One of the key ways to support small businesses in urban settings is by fostering an enabling economic environment that promotes their success.

First and foremost, it is crucial to enhance access to capital and financial resources. Many small businesses struggle to secure funding due to limited credit history or collateral. By collaborating with financial institutions and creating micro-lending programs, we can provide the necessary financial support to help these businesses thrive. Additionally, offering financial literacy programs can equip entrepreneurs with the knowledge and skills to manage their finances effectively.

Furthermore, streamlining the regulatory and licensing processes is essential. Small businesses often face bureaucratic hurdles that can hinder their growth. By simplifying these processes and reducing red tape, we can encourage entrepreneurship and enable small businesses to focus on their core operations rather than navigating complex administrative procedures.

Collaboration and networking opportunities are also vital for small businesses in urban environments. By creating platforms for knowledge sharing, mentorship, and collaboration, we can foster a sense of community and provide small business owners with the support they need. Local chambers of commerce and business associations can play a crucial role in facilitating these connections and promoting collaboration.

Lastly, promoting small businesses through marketing and public awareness campaigns can have a significant impact. By highlighting the unique offerings of these businesses, we can attract more customers, drive foot traffic to urban areas, and ultimately contribute to the economic growth of our cities.

In conclusion, supporting small businesses in urban environments is crucial for fostering economic growth and creating vibrant communities. By enhancing access to capital, streamlining regulations, facilitating collaboration, and promoting public awareness, we can create an enabling economic environment that empowers small businesses to thrive. As individuals, we can play an active role in supporting these businesses by shopping locally, spreading the word, and engaging in initiatives that promote their growth. Together, let's make a difference and ensure the success of small businesses in our urban environments.

Chapter 7: Urban Economic Opportunities for All

Inclusive Economic Development Strategies

In today's rapidly changing economic environment, it is crucial to adopt inclusive economic development strategies that benefit everyone. As our cities continue to grow and evolve, it is imperative that we prioritize the well-being and prosperity of all individuals, regardless of their backgrounds or circumstances. In this subchapter, we will delve into the importance of inclusive economic development and explore various strategies that can be implemented to foster a more equitable and thriving urban economy.

Inclusive economic development aims to create opportunities and ensure that the benefits of economic growth are shared by all members of society. It recognizes that a thriving economy cannot be achieved if certain segments of the population are left behind. By embracing inclusivity, cities can tap into the vast potential of their diverse populations and foster innovation, creativity, and resilience.

One of the key strategies for inclusive economic development is promoting equal access to education and skills training. By investing in quality education, vocational training, and lifelong learning opportunities, cities can equip individuals with the necessary tools to participate in and contribute to the economy. This includes providing affordable and accessible education for all age groups and empowering marginalized communities to overcome barriers to education.

Another important aspect of inclusive economic development is fostering entrepreneurship and supporting small and medium-sized enterprises (SMEs). By creating an enabling environment for entrepreneurship, cities can encourage innovation and job creation. This can be achieved through providing access to capital, mentorship programs, and reducing bureaucratic hurdles for starting and scaling businesses. Additionally, ensuring that business support services are accessible to diverse groups, including women and minority entrepreneurs, can help level the playing field and promote economic inclusion.

Furthermore, inclusive economic development requires addressing systemic barriers and promoting social cohesion. This entails tackling issues such as discrimination, income inequality, and affordable housing. By implementing policies that promote fair employment practices, affordable housing initiatives, and social safety nets, cities can create an environment that supports economic mobility and reduces disparities.

In conclusion, inclusive economic development is essential for creating sustainable and resilient urban economies. By ensuring equal access to education, supporting entrepreneurship, and addressing systemic barriers, cities can foster an environment where everyone can thrive and contribute to economic growth. It is time to embrace inclusive economic development strategies and pave the way towards a more equitable and prosperous future for all.

Enhancing Financial Literacy in Urban Communities

In today's rapidly changing economic environment, financial literacy has become more crucial than ever before. As we navigate the urban economic landscape, it is essential for everyone, regardless of their background or profession, to have a solid understanding of financial concepts and the tools necessary to make informed decisions about their money. This subchapter of "Money Moves: Navigating the Urban Economic Landscape" aims to address the importance of enhancing financial literacy in urban communities and provide practical tips to empower individuals and families to take control of their financial futures.

Urban communities often face unique challenges when it comes to financial literacy. Limited access to quality education, income inequality, and a lack of financial resources can hinder individuals from developing the necessary skills to make wise financial choices. However, by addressing these challenges head-on, we can empower urban communities to build a strong financial foundation and achieve economic success.

This subchapter will explore various strategies to enhance financial literacy in urban communities. It will highlight the importance of education, both formal and informal, as a means to empower individuals and equip them with the knowledge and skills to manage their finances effectively. It will emphasize the significance of fostering a culture of saving, budgeting, and investing, helping individuals to develop healthy financial habits that will serve them well in the long run.

Furthermore, this subchapter will shed light on the importance of community engagement and collaboration. By establishing partnerships between local governments, educational institutions, and community organizations, we can create a support network that provides accessible resources and financial education programs tailored to the needs of urban communities. These efforts will not only enhance financial literacy but also promote economic growth and stability within these communities.

Throughout this subchapter, practical tips and tools will be provided to help individuals navigate the complexities of personal finance in an urban setting. Topics such as managing debt, understanding credit scores, and making informed investment decisions will be explored in an accessible and engaging manner. By demystifying these concepts and providing actionable advice, readers will be equipped with the tools necessary to make sound financial decisions that will positively impact their lives.

In conclusion, enhancing financial literacy in urban communities is a crucial step towards empowering individuals and promoting economic growth. By addressing the unique challenges faced by urban communities and providing accessible resources and education, we can equip individuals with the knowledge and skills necessary to navigate the urban economic landscape successfully. This subchapter aims to inspire and guide readers on their journey towards financial empowerment, regardless of their background or profession.

Creating Economic Opportunities for Marginalized Groups

In today's rapidly changing economic environment, it is crucial to address the issue of economic inequality and create opportunities for marginalized groups. In this subchapter, we will explore the various ways in which we can empower these groups, promote inclusivity, and foster economic growth for everyone.

1. Education and Skill Development: One of the key factors that hinder economic opportunities for marginalized groups is the lack of access to quality education and skill development. By investing in educational programs and vocational training, we can equip individuals from marginalized communities with the necessary skills to thrive in the urban economic landscape. This could include initiatives such as scholarships, mentorship programs, and partnerships with educational institutions.

2. Entrepreneurship and Small Business Support: Encouraging entrepreneurship and providing support to small businesses is vital in creating economic opportunities for marginalized groups. By offering resources, training, and access to capital, we can empower individuals to start their own businesses and contribute to the local economy. Additionally, fostering networking opportunities and creating platforms for collaboration can help marginalized entrepreneurs connect with potential investors and customers.

3. Diversity and Inclusion in Corporate Culture: To truly create economic opportunities, we must address the systemic barriers that exist within the corporate world. Companies should actively promote diversity and inclusion by implementing unbiased

hiring practices, offering equal pay and advancement opportunities, and providing inclusive work environments. By breaking down these barriers, marginalized groups can access better job prospects, higher wages, and meaningful career growth.

4. Community Development and Investment: Investing in marginalized communities is crucial for their economic growth. This could involve revitalizing infrastructure, improving access to essential services like healthcare and transportation, and supporting community-driven initiatives. By focusing on community development, we can create a conducive environment for economic opportunities to flourish.

5. Policy and Advocacy: Creating lasting change requires policy reforms and advocacy efforts. Governments and policymakers should prioritize policies that promote economic inclusivity, such as targeted tax incentives for businesses in marginalized areas and the implementation of anti-discrimination laws. Additionally, advocacy groups and organizations can raise awareness, lobby for change, and hold corporations and governments accountable for their actions.

In conclusion, creating economic opportunities for marginalized groups is not only a moral imperative but also essential for the overall economic health of our society. By investing in education, entrepreneurship, diversity, community development, and policy reforms, we can pave the way for a more inclusive and prosperous urban economic landscape. Empowering marginalized groups will not only benefit them but also contribute to the growth and vibrancy of the entire economic environment.

Chapter 8: Navigating the Urban Job Market

Job Search Strategies in Urban Areas

In today's competitive job market, finding employment in urban areas can be both daunting and challenging. With a high concentration of job seekers and limited opportunities, it is crucial to develop effective job search strategies to navigate the urban economic landscape successfully. This subchapter aims to provide valuable insights and practical tips for individuals from all walks of life to enhance their job search efforts in urban areas.

Understanding the economic environment of urban areas is the first step towards a successful job search. Urban areas are characterized by a diverse range of industries, including finance, technology, healthcare, and creative sectors. By researching and identifying the industries that thrive in urban areas, job seekers can align their skills and experiences with the demands of the local job market.

Networking is an indispensable tool for job seekers in urban areas. Building a strong professional network can open doors to hidden job opportunities and provide valuable insights into the job market. Attending industry-specific events, joining professional organizations, and leveraging online platforms like LinkedIn can help individuals connect with influential people in their field and gain access to job leads.

Leveraging technology is another crucial aspect of job search strategies in urban areas. Online job boards, company websites, and social media platforms can serve as valuable resources for finding job openings. Job seekers should regularly update their online profiles, tailor their resumes to specific job postings, and actively engage with potential employers through online platforms to increase their visibility and chances of being noticed.

Additionally, it is essential to consider alternative job search methods in urban areas. Traditional approaches like cold-calling, door-to-door visits, and informational interviews can still be effective in establishing connections and uncovering hidden job opportunities. Furthermore, considering part-time or temporary positions, internships, or freelance work can provide valuable experience, expand professional networks, and potentially lead to full-time employment opportunities.

In conclusion, job search strategies in urban areas require a multifaceted approach that encompasses understanding the economic environment, networking, leveraging technology, and considering alternative methods. By adopting these strategies, individuals from all backgrounds can navigate the urban economic landscape with confidence and increase their chances of finding meaningful employment. Remember, perseverance, adaptability, and a proactive mindset are key to success in today's urban job market.

Skills and Education for Urban Employment

In today's rapidly evolving economic environment, acquiring the right skills and education is crucial for securing employment in urban areas. As the cities continue to grow and transform, so do the requirements of the job market. It is essential for individuals, regardless of their background or current employment status, to stay ahead of these changes to navigate the urban economic landscape successfully.

One of the primary reasons why skills and education are vital for urban employment is the increasing demand for specialized knowledge. Urban areas are often hubs of innovation and technological advancements, which means that industries are constantly evolving. As new technologies emerge and industries adapt, individuals who possess the necessary skills and education in these areas will have a competitive edge in the job market.

Moreover, urban areas are often characterized by a diverse and multicultural population, resulting in a highly competitive job market. Being equipped with relevant skills and education can help individuals stand out among their peers. Employers are increasingly looking for candidates who possess a diverse skill set and can adapt to the changing needs of the urban workforce.

Investing in skills and education also opens up opportunities for career advancement and higher earning potential. Urban areas tend to offer a wide range of job opportunities, but many of these positions require specialized knowledge or advanced degrees. By continuously improving and expanding one's skill set, individuals can position themselves for higher-paying jobs and increase their chances of career growth.

Fortunately, there are various avenues available for individuals to acquire the necessary skills and education for urban employment. Traditional educational institutions, such as universities and colleges, offer degree programs and specialized courses that cater to the needs of urban industries. Additionally, online platforms and vocational schools provide flexible learning options, allowing individuals to gain skills at their own pace.

To make the most of these opportunities, individuals should also consider networking and seeking mentorship within their chosen industries. Engaging with professionals in the field can provide valuable insights and connections that can enhance career prospects in urban areas.

In conclusion, skills and education play a vital role in securing employment in the urban economic environment. As cities continue to evolve, specialized knowledge, adaptability, and a diverse skill set become increasingly important. By investing in continuous learning and staying ahead of industry trends, individuals can position themselves for success in the competitive job market of urban areas. Whether through traditional educational institutions or online platforms, individuals should seize the available opportunities to acquire the skills and education needed to navigate the urban economic landscape successfully.

Thriving in the Gig Economy: Urban Freelancing

In today's rapidly changing economic environment, traditional employment models are being challenged by the rise of the gig economy. The gig economy refers to a labor market characterized by short-term contracts, freelance work, and independent contracting. This shift has been particularly prominent in urban areas, where a multitude of opportunities exist for individuals to leverage their skills and talents to earn a living.

Urban freelancing offers a unique set of advantages for those seeking flexible work arrangements. One of the primary benefits is the ability to work on multiple projects simultaneously, allowing freelancers to diversify their income streams and reduce the risk of relying on a single employer. This flexibility also enables individuals to pursue their passions and develop a portfolio career, where they can combine various skills and interests to create a fulfilling and dynamic work life.

Another advantage of urban freelancing is the potential for higher earnings. By working independently, freelancers have the freedom to set their rates and negotiate contracts based on their expertise and market demand. Additionally, urban areas often offer a larger customer base and a higher density of businesses, increasing the potential for finding well-paying gigs.

However, thriving in the gig economy requires a proactive approach and a set of essential skills. Self-promotion and marketing become crucial in order to stand out in a competitive market. Building a strong online presence through websites, social media platforms, and professional networks can help freelancers establish their credibility and attract clients.

Time management is another vital skill for urban freelancers. With multiple projects and clients, it is essential to prioritize tasks, meet deadlines, and maintain a healthy work-life balance. Setting clear boundaries and establishing a routine can help freelancers stay organized and maximize productivity.

Additionally, freelancers need to be financially savvy. Since they are responsible for their own taxes, insurance, and retirement savings, it is crucial to plan for these expenses and manage income effectively. Creating a budget and setting aside funds for emergency situations is essential to ensure long-term financial stability.

The gig economy offers immense opportunities for individuals to thrive in the urban economic landscape. By embracing the flexibility, independence, and potential for higher earnings, freelancers can carve out a successful and fulfilling career. However, it is important to develop the necessary skills, stay adaptable, and continuously invest in personal and professional growth to navigate the ever-evolving gig economy successfully.

Chapter 9: Investing in the Urban Economy

Real Estate Investment in Urban Areas

In today's urban economic environment, real estate investment has become an increasingly popular avenue for individuals and businesses looking to grow their wealth. The allure of urban areas lies in the potential for high returns and the numerous opportunities that come with investing in properties located in bustling cities.

One of the key advantages of real estate investment in urban areas is the potential for long-term appreciation. Urban areas are often characterized by high demand for housing and commercial spaces, leading to an increase in property values over time. As cities continue to grow and attract more people, the demand for real estate in these areas is likely to remain strong, making it an attractive investment option.

Investing in urban real estate also offers the opportunity for generating passive income. Rental properties in urban areas tend to have higher rental rates due to the demand for housing. This means that investors can enjoy a steady stream of income as tenants rent their properties. With proper management and maintenance, real estate investments can provide a reliable source of income for many years to come.

Furthermore, real estate investment allows individuals to diversify their investment portfolio. While other forms of investment, such as stocks and bonds, may be subject to market volatility, real estate investments tend to be more stable in the long run. By adding real estate assets to their portfolio, investors can reduce their exposure to risks associated with fluctuations in the stock market and economic downturns.

Investing in urban areas also provides the opportunity to be part of the revitalization and development of a city. As urban areas continue to evolve, there are often government initiatives and private sector investments aimed at improving infrastructure and creating new business opportunities. By investing in real estate in these areas, individuals can contribute to the economic growth of the city while also benefiting from the potential increase in property values.

However, it is important to note that real estate investment in urban areas also comes with its own set of challenges. The high cost of properties in urban areas can be a barrier to entry for some investors. Additionally, managing properties in urban areas may require more time and effort due to the higher turnover of tenants and the need for regular maintenance.

In conclusion, real estate investment in urban areas offers a wealth of opportunities for individuals and businesses looking to navigate the urban economic landscape. From the potential for long-term appreciation to generating passive income and diversifying investment portfolios, urban real estate investment can be a lucrative venture. By carefully considering the risks and rewards associated with investing in urban areas, individuals can make informed decisions that align with their financial goals and contribute to the economic growth of vibrant cities.

Stock Market and Urban Economic Trends

In today's globalized world, the stock market plays a crucial role in shaping urban economic trends. The stock market is a complex system where individuals and institutions buy and sell shares of publicly traded companies. It serves as a barometer for the overall health of the economy and influences the decision-making process of businesses, investors, and consumers alike. Understanding the stock market and its impact on urban economic trends is essential for navigating the ever-changing urban economic landscape.

One of the key ways in which the stock market influences urban economic trends is through its effect on investor confidence. When the stock market is performing well, investors tend to be more optimistic about the future prospects of the economy. This optimism leads to increased investment in businesses and industries, stimulating economic growth and job creation in urban areas. On the other hand, a decline in the stock market can instill fear and uncertainty among investors, leading to a decrease in investment and economic activity.

Moreover, the stock market serves as a source of capital for businesses, particularly those based in urban areas. Companies often raise funds by selling shares to the public through initial public offerings (IPOs). This influx of capital allows businesses to expand their operations, invest in research and development, and create new jobs. The success or failure of these IPOs can have a significant impact on the economic landscape of urban areas, attracting or deterring businesses from establishing themselves in a particular city.

Furthermore, the stock market provides a platform for urban dwellers to participate in the economy as investors. Individuals can invest in stocks, either directly or through mutual funds and retirement accounts, to grow their wealth and secure their financial future. By understanding the dynamics of the stock market, individuals can make informed investment decisions that align with their financial goals.

It is important to note that the stock market is not a perfect reflection of the entire economy. However, it is a valuable tool for understanding and analyzing urban economic trends. By monitoring stock market indices, such as the Dow Jones Industrial Average or the S&P 500, individuals can gain insights into the overall health of the economy and make informed decisions regarding their personal finances.

In conclusion, the stock market plays a pivotal role in shaping urban economic trends. Its impact on investor confidence, capital formation for businesses, and opportunities for individual investors cannot be understated. Understanding the stock market and its relationship with urban economic trends is crucial for everyone, as it allows for informed decision-making in an ever-evolving economic environment.

Impact Investing and Socially Responsible Urban Development

In recent years, the concept of impact investing has gained significant attention as a means of promoting positive change in urban environments. This approach to investment focuses on generating both financial returns and social or environmental impact. It represents a shift in the way we think about economic growth, recognizing that it is not enough to simply pursue profits; we must also consider the well-being of our communities and the planet.

Impact investing in the context of urban development aims to address the complex challenges faced by cities around the world. From affordable housing and transportation to sustainable energy and job creation, these issues require innovative solutions that traditional investment models may not prioritize. By directing capital towards projects that deliver both financial and societal benefits, impact investors can play a crucial role in shaping the future of our urban landscapes.

One key aspect of impact investing in urban development is the emphasis on socially responsible practices. This means investing in projects that prioritize the needs and aspirations of local communities, particularly those that have historically been marginalized or underserved. By actively engaging with residents and stakeholders, impact investors can ensure that their investments align with the values and priorities of the people they aim to serve.

Furthermore, impact investing in urban development often involves a long-term perspective. Rather than seeking short-term gains, investors committed to social responsibility recognize that sustainable and inclusive urban development requires patience and persistence. This approach encourages collaboration between stakeholders, including public and private entities, to achieve shared goals and create lasting positive change.

The economic environment benefits from impact investing in urban development in several ways. First, it stimulates economic growth by creating jobs and fostering entrepreneurship in underserved communities. By investing in local businesses and infrastructure, impact investors can help revitalize struggling neighborhoods and promote economic self-sufficiency.

Second, impact investing contributes to the overall well-being of urban residents. Investments in affordable housing, healthcare facilities, and education can improve quality of life and enhance social mobility. Moreover, by prioritizing sustainability and environmental responsibility, impact investors help create healthier and more resilient cities that can withstand the challenges of the future.

In conclusion, impact investing and socially responsible urban development are powerful tools for addressing the economic and social challenges faced by cities today. By integrating financial returns with positive social and environmental impact, impact investors can drive positive change and create more equitable and sustainable urban landscapes. As we navigate the complex urban economic landscape, it is crucial that we all recognize the potential of impact investing to shape a better future for everyone.

Chapter 10: Financial Planning for Urban Living

Budgeting and Managing Urban Living Expenses

Living in a bustling urban environment comes with its own set of challenges, especially when it comes to managing your finances. In this subchapter, we will explore different strategies and tips for budgeting and effectively managing your urban living expenses. Whether you are a young professional, a family, or a retiree, these principles can be applied to anyone living in an urban economic environment.

Creating a budget is the first step towards financial stability in an urban setting. Begin by assessing your income and categorizing your expenses. Urban living often involves higher costs for housing, transportation, and entertainment. It is crucial to allocate a suitable amount of your income to these categories while still leaving room for savings and emergencies.

When it comes to housing, evaluate your options and choose the most affordable one that meets your needs. Consider factors such as rent or mortgage payments, utilities, and maintenance costs. Urban areas may have various housing options, including apartments, condos, or shared living spaces. By carefully analyzing your budget, you can make an informed decision that aligns with your financial goals.

Transportation is another significant expense in urban areas. Assess your commuting needs and explore cost-effective options such as public transportation, carpooling, or cycling. Many cities also offer bike-sharing programs, which can be an efficient and eco-friendly way to get around.

Entertainment and dining out are often tempting in urban environments, but they can quickly drain your bank account. Set a reasonable budget for these activities and prioritize experiences that offer good value for your money. Look for free or low-cost events, explore local parks, and seek out affordable dining options to maintain a healthy balance between enjoyment and financial stability.

Additionally, managing your urban living expenses requires careful monitoring of your finances. Utilize technology to track your expenses, set financial goals, and receive alerts for bill payments. Many budgeting apps are available that can simplify this process and provide a clear overview of your spending habits.

Remember, budgeting is an ongoing process. Regularly review and adjust your budget as your circumstances change. By prioritizing your spending, making conscious choices, and staying disciplined, you can successfully navigate the urban economic landscape and achieve financial well-being in any economic environment.

Saving and Investing in an Urban Environment

In today's fast-paced urban environment, it is becoming increasingly essential to understand the importance of saving and investing. With the constant hustle and bustle, it can be easy to fall into the trap of living paycheck to paycheck, but taking control of your finances is crucial for long-term stability and prosperity. This subchapter explores various strategies and considerations for saving and investing in an urban setting, equipping readers with the knowledge to navigate the complex economic landscape successfully.

One of the first steps in saving and investing is creating a budget. In an urban environment, where the cost of living can be higher, tracking your expenses becomes even more crucial. By creating a comprehensive budget that outlines your income and expenses, you can identify areas where you can cut back and save more. This budgeting practice allows you to allocate funds towards investments and build a solid financial foundation.

Another key aspect of saving and investing in an urban environment is understanding the different investment options available. From stocks and bonds to real estate and mutual funds, there are various avenues to consider. It is essential to educate yourself about the potential risks and returns associated with each investment type, ensuring that you make informed decisions that align with your financial goals.

Furthermore, in an urban environment, where opportunities to save money may be limited, it is crucial to seek out alternative ways to save. This could include exploring local community programs, such as shared housing or co-ops, which can help reduce living expenses.

Additionally, taking advantage of public transportation or car-sharing services can significantly cut down on transportation costs.

It is also important to diversify your investment portfolio and consider long-term financial goals. Urban environments offer unique investment opportunities, such as investing in local startups or supporting sustainable urban development projects. By diversifying your investments, you can minimize risks and maximize potential returns.

Lastly, staying informed about the ever-changing economic landscape is vital. Urban environments are dynamic, with economic trends and policies that can impact your savings and investments. Stay updated with financial news, attend seminars or workshops, and consider consulting with a financial advisor to ensure you make well-informed decisions that align with your goals.

Saving and investing in an urban environment may seem challenging, but with careful planning and strategic decision-making, it is entirely possible to build a secure financial future. Take control of your finances, create a budget, explore various investment options, and stay informed about the economic landscape. By doing so, you can navigate the urban economic landscape successfully and achieve financial stability and prosperity.

Retirement Planning in the Urban Setting

In today's fast-paced urban environment, retirement planning has become more important than ever. With the constantly changing economic landscape, it is crucial for individuals from all walks of life to carefully consider their financial future. This subchapter aims to provide valuable insights and guidance on retirement planning specifically tailored to the urban setting.

Retirement planning in the urban environment comes with its own unique set of challenges and opportunities. The economic environment in cities is often characterized by higher living costs, increased competition, and fluctuating job markets. Therefore, it is vital for individuals to understand how these factors can impact their retirement savings and develop strategies to overcome them.

One key aspect of retirement planning in the urban setting is understanding the importance of starting early. With the rising cost of living in cities, it is essential to begin saving as soon as possible to ensure a comfortable retirement. This subchapter will delve into the various retirement savings options available, such as employer-sponsored retirement plans, individual retirement accounts (IRAs), and other investment vehicles that can help individuals build a robust retirement nest egg.

Additionally, this subchapter will emphasize the significance of budgeting and managing expenses effectively in an urban environment. It will provide practical tips on how to strike a balance between enjoying the urban lifestyle and saving for retirement. Urban dwellers will learn how to prioritize their spending, cut unnecessary expenses, and make wise financial decisions that align with their long-term retirement goals.

Furthermore, this subchapter will explore the potential benefits and drawbacks of retiring in an urban setting. It will discuss various factors individuals should consider when deciding whether to remain in the city during retirement or relocate to a more affordable location. It will also shed light on the potential challenges and opportunities urban retirees may face, such as access to healthcare, social activities, and housing options.

In conclusion, retirement planning in the urban setting requires careful consideration of the economic environment and unique challenges faced by city dwellers. This subchapter aims to provide valuable insights and practical advice to help individuals navigate the urban economic landscape and secure a financially stable retirement. By understanding the importance of early savings, effective budgeting, and weighing the pros and cons of retiring in an urban environment, readers will be empowered to make informed decisions and achieve their retirement goals.

Chapter 11: Overcoming Financial Challenges in the Urban Landscape

Dealing with Urban Debt and Financial Stress

In today's urban economic environment, many individuals and families find themselves grappling with the burden of debt and financial stress. The fast-paced urban lifestyle, coupled with rising living costs, can often lead to a precarious financial situation. However, it is essential to remember that you are not alone in this struggle. This subchapter aims to provide practical strategies and advice for dealing with urban debt and financial stress, helping you navigate your way to a more stable financial future.

The first step in tackling urban debt is to gain a clear understanding of your financial situation. Take the time to review your income, expenses, and debts. Creating a budget can be a powerful tool to track your spending and identify areas where you can cut back. Consider seeking the help of a financial advisor or credit counselor who can provide expert guidance tailored to your specific circumstances.

When it comes to managing debt, it is crucial to prioritize high-interest debts and develop a plan to pay them off systematically. Explore debt consolidation options that can help you reduce interest rates and simplify your repayment process. It is also essential to resist the temptation of taking on additional debt while working towards financial stability.

In dealing with financial stress, it is crucial to maintain a healthy mindset. Understand that financial setbacks are a common part of life, and there are steps you can take to overcome them. Surround yourself with a supportive network of friends and family who can offer encouragement and advice. Additionally, consider exploring stress-relief techniques such as meditation, exercise, or engaging in hobbies that bring you joy.

Taking control of your urban financial situation also involves seeking out resources and opportunities available to you. Research local community programs that offer financial education workshops or assistance with debt management. Take advantage of government programs that provide subsidies for housing, food, or healthcare, if applicable.

Remember, overcoming urban debt and financial stress requires perseverance and determination. It may take time to see significant progress, but every small step counts. By adopting sound financial habits, seeking assistance when needed, and staying committed to your financial goals, you can pave the way for a brighter and more secure future.

In conclusion, "Dealing with Urban Debt and Financial Stress" provides valuable insights into navigating the urban economic landscape. By implementing the strategies outlined in this subchapter, individuals from all walks of life can take control of their financial situation and work towards a more stable and prosperous future.

Strategies for Overcoming Urban Financial Barriers

In today's rapidly changing economic environment, urban communities face numerous financial barriers that can hinder their growth and prosperity. These barriers often include limited access to affordable housing, education, healthcare, and employment opportunities. To address these challenges, individuals and communities must adopt effective strategies that empower them to overcome urban financial barriers and achieve economic stability. In this subchapter, we will explore some practical strategies that can help navigate the urban economic landscape and create positive money moves for everyone.

1. Financial Education: A strong foundation in financial literacy is essential for individuals to make informed decisions about their money. Communities should prioritize offering workshops, seminars, and programs that teach basic financial skills, such as budgeting, saving, and investing. By equipping individuals with the knowledge and tools they need to manage their finances effectively, we can empower them to overcome financial barriers.

2. Collaboration and Networking: Building strong networks and collaborations within the community is crucial for overcoming financial barriers. By connecting with local organizations, businesses, and government agencies, individuals can access resources, job opportunities, and financial assistance programs. Collaboration also fosters community support and empowers individuals to pool their resources and knowledge to tackle common financial challenges.

3. Entrepreneurship and Small Business Development: Encouraging entrepreneurship and supporting small business development can create economic opportunities within urban communities. By providing training, mentorship, and access to capital, individuals can start their own businesses and generate income, thereby reducing financial barriers and creating job opportunities for others.

4. Affordable Housing Initiatives: Access to affordable housing is a critical issue in many urban areas. Governments, nonprofit organizations, and community leaders should work together to develop affordable housing initiatives, such as subsidized rental programs, low-cost mortgage options, and affordable housing cooperatives. These initiatives can help individuals and families secure stable housing, reduce their financial burden, and improve their overall financial well-being.

5. Advocacy and Policy Change: Overcoming urban financial barriers requires advocating for policy changes that address systemic issues. Individuals and communities should engage in advocacy efforts to influence local, state, and federal policies that promote economic equity, access to quality education, healthcare, and job opportunities.

By implementing these strategies, we can create a more inclusive and supportive economic environment for everyone. Overcoming urban financial barriers is a collective effort that requires collaboration, education, and policy change. Together, we can navigate the urban economic landscape and empower individuals and communities to achieve financial success and prosperity.

Building Resilience in the Face of Urban Economic Challenges

In an ever-changing economic landscape, cities are at the forefront of economic growth and development. However, they also face numerous challenges that can disrupt their economic stability. From globalization and rapid technological advancements to economic recessions and social inequalities, urban areas must find ways to build resilience and adapt to these challenges in order to thrive.

Resilience in the face of economic challenges is not about simply surviving, but rather thriving and prospering in the midst of adversity. It requires a proactive approach and a comprehensive understanding of the economic environment. This subchapter aims to provide valuable insights and practical strategies to help individuals and communities navigate the urban economic landscape and build resilience.

One key aspect of building resilience is understanding the economic environment. This includes examining the global and local factors that influence urban economies, such as trade policies, market trends, and demographic changes. By staying informed and aware of these factors, individuals can anticipate and prepare for potential economic challenges.

Furthermore, building resilience requires a multidimensional approach that encompasses both individual and community levels. Individuals must cultivate a mindset of adaptability and continuous learning to remain competitive in the job market. This may involve acquiring new skills, pursuing higher education, or exploring entrepreneurship opportunities. Additionally, fostering a strong social support network and engaging in community initiatives can enhance resilience by promoting collaboration and resource sharing.

At the community level, building resilience involves creating economic diversification and promoting inclusive growth. Cities should invest in infrastructure development, innovation hubs, and sustainable industries to attract new businesses and create employment opportunities. Moreover, fostering social inclusivity and reducing inequalities can enhance the overall economic resilience of a city, as it ensures that everyone has equal access to economic resources and opportunities.

Lastly, building resilience requires effective governance and policy implementation. Governments and local authorities play a crucial role in creating an enabling environment for economic growth and resilience. This includes implementing robust financial regulations, supporting small and medium-sized enterprises, and investing in education and healthcare. Additionally, governments should prioritize sustainability and resilience in their urban planning and infrastructure development to mitigate the risks of economic shocks and natural disasters.

In conclusion, building resilience in the face of urban economic challenges is essential for individuals and communities to thrive in today's rapidly changing economic landscape. By understanding the economic environment, adopting an adaptable mindset, fostering social inclusivity, and implementing effective governance, cities can overcome challenges and create a sustainable and prosperous future for all.

Chapter 12: The Future of Urban Economics

Emerging Trends and Technologies in Urban Economies

In today's rapidly changing world, urban economies are at the forefront of innovation and development. As cities become increasingly interconnected, the economic landscape is evolving in response to emerging trends and technologies. This subchapter explores the transformative impact of these advancements on the economic environment, highlighting the opportunities and challenges they present for individuals and businesses alike.

One of the most significant trends shaping urban economies is the rise of the digital age. With the advent of the internet and the proliferation of smartphones, cities are becoming smart hubs, integrating technology into every aspect of urban life. From smart transportation systems that optimize traffic flow to digital marketplaces that connect consumers and producers, technology is revolutionizing the way we live and do business.

The sharing economy is another emerging trend that is reshaping urban economies. Platforms like Airbnb and Uber have disrupted traditional industries, enabling individuals to monetize their assets and skills. This new model of peer-to-peer exchange is not only driving economic growth but also fostering a sense of community and collaboration in cities.

Artificial intelligence (AI) and automation are also having a profound impact on urban economies. As AI technologies continue to advance, they are transforming industries, from manufacturing to finance.

While automation may lead to job displacement in some sectors, it also presents new opportunities for innovation and the creation of new jobs. Skill development and retraining will be crucial to ensure that individuals can adapt to these changes and remain competitive in the job market.

Sustainability and environmental consciousness are becoming increasingly important in urban economies. As cities grapple with the challenges of climate change and resource scarcity, they are embracing renewable energy, green infrastructure, and circular economy principles. These initiatives not only reduce environmental impact but also create new economic opportunities, such as the growth of clean technology industries and the development of sustainable urban planning practices.

The emergence of blockchain technology and cryptocurrencies is another trend that is reshaping urban economies. Blockchain has the potential to revolutionize financial systems, supply chains, and governance structures, enabling secure and transparent transactions without the need for intermediaries. Cryptocurrencies, such as Bitcoin, are challenging traditional notions of money and finance, offering new avenues for investment and economic exchange.

As urban economies continue to evolve, it is essential for individuals and businesses to stay informed about these emerging trends and technologies. Adapting to these changes will require a willingness to embrace new ideas, acquire new skills, and foster a culture of innovation and collaboration. By doing so, we can navigate the urban economic landscape and harness the potential of these trends and technologies to create thriving and sustainable cities for everyone.

Forecasting the Future of Urban Development

In this subchapter, we delve into the exciting world of urban development and explore the potential future trends that will shape our cities. The economic environment is constantly evolving, and it is crucial for everyone to understand the trajectory of urban development to make informed decisions.

As we step into an era defined by rapid urbanization, the future of urban development holds both opportunities and challenges. With the world population projected to reach 9.7 billion by 2050, cities will face immense pressure to accommodate the growing numbers. This will require innovative solutions that focus on sustainable and inclusive development.

One of the key trends we anticipate is the rise of smart cities. With advancements in technology, cities are becoming more connected, efficient, and livable. Smart infrastructure, such as intelligent transportation systems and energy-efficient buildings, will enhance the quality of life for urban dwellers. Additionally, the integration of Internet of Things (IoT) devices will enable cities to collect real-time data, optimizing resource allocation and improving urban services.

Another significant development on the horizon is the emphasis on green and resilient cities. Climate change and environmental concerns have become urgent issues, demanding cities to adopt sustainable practices. Urban planners will increasingly prioritize green spaces, renewable energy sources, and sustainable transportation options. By incorporating nature into urban landscapes, we can create healthier and more livable cities for all.

Furthermore, the future of urban development will witness a shift towards mixed-use developments. Traditional city planning separated residential, commercial, and recreational areas. However, future cities will embrace mixed-use zoning, creating vibrant neighborhoods where people can live, work, and play in close proximity. This integration will reduce commuting times and foster a sense of community and belonging.

As the global economy continues to evolve, urban development will also be influenced by economic trends. We anticipate a rise in knowledge-based economies, where cities will prioritize education, research, and innovation. By nurturing a skilled workforce and providing a conducive environment for startups and entrepreneurs, cities can attract investment and foster economic growth.

In conclusion, the future of urban development holds immense potential for economic and environmental transformation. It is essential for everyone to understand these trends and actively participate in shaping the cities we live in. By embracing smart technologies, sustainability, mixed-use developments, and knowledge-based economies, we can create inclusive, resilient, and prosperous urban environments for generations to come.

Creating Sustainable and Equitable Urban Economies

In today's rapidly changing world, it is crucial to address the challenges associated with urban economies. As cities continue to expand and evolve, it is essential to create sustainable and equitable urban economies that benefit everyone. This subchapter aims to explore the strategies and approaches that can be taken to navigate the urban economic landscape, ensuring a prosperous future for all.

Sustainability lies at the heart of building resilient urban economies. With the increasing threat of climate change and resource depletion, it is vital to prioritize sustainable practices. This involves promoting renewable energy sources, encouraging environmentally friendly transportation options, and implementing green infrastructure. By embracing sustainable solutions, cities can reduce their carbon footprint and contribute to a healthier planet.

Equity is another crucial aspect of creating urban economies that work for everyone. Economic disparities can lead to social unrest and hinder overall progress. To address this, policies must be designed to promote equal opportunities and reduce income inequality. This can be achieved through inclusive growth strategies that focus on providing access to education, healthcare, and affordable housing. By ensuring that everyone has a fair chance to participate in and benefit from the urban economy, cities can foster social cohesion and harmony.

Furthermore, investing in innovation and technology can serve as a catalyst for economic growth in urban environments. By embracing digitalization and fostering a culture of entrepreneurship, cities can attract businesses, create jobs, and stimulate economic development.

Additionally, supporting small and medium-sized enterprises (SMEs) can foster local entrepreneurship and strengthen the urban economy from within.

Collaboration and cooperation between various stakeholders are also crucial for the success of sustainable and equitable urban economies. Governments, businesses, community organizations, and citizens must work together to develop and implement strategies that promote economic prosperity while considering the needs and aspirations of all.

In conclusion, creating sustainable and equitable urban economies is a multifaceted endeavor that requires a holistic approach. By prioritizing sustainability, promoting equity, embracing innovation, and fostering collaboration, cities can navigate the urban economic landscape successfully. This subchapter seeks to inspire and empower readers to take action and contribute to the creation of prosperous, inclusive, and environmentally conscious urban economies for the benefit of all.

www.ingramcontent.com/pod-product-compliance
Lightning Source LLC
LaVergne TN
LVHW052000060526
838201LV00059B/3753